THE

WYATT

PROVERBS

EXHORTATIONS IN POETRY

By MEL WYATT

WestBow Press books may be ordered through booksellers or by contacting:

WestBow Press
A Division of Thomas Nelson & Zondervan
1663 Liberty Drive
Bloomington, IN 47403
www.westbowpress.com
1 (866) 928-1240

Because of the dynamic nature of the Internet, any web addresses or links contained in this book may have changed since publication and may no longer be valid. The views expressed in this work are solely those of the author and do not necessarily reflect the views of the publisher, and the publisher hereby disclaims any responsibility for them.

Scripture quotations taken from the New American Standard Bible®, Copyright © 1960, 1962, 1963, 1968, 1971, 1972, 1973, 1975, 1977, 1995 by The Lockman Foundation. Used by permission. (www.Lockman.org)

Any people depicted in stock imagery provided by Thinkstock are models, and such images are being used for illustrative purposes only.
Certain stock imagery © Thinkstock.

ISBN: 978-1-4908-3421-4 (sc)
ISBN: 978-1-4908-3422-1 (e)

Library of Congress Control Number: 2014906969

Printed in the United States of America.

WestBow Press rev. date: 5/7/2014

WestBow
PRESS
A DIVISION OF THOMAS NELSON
& ZONDERVAN

In Dedication
To my dear Christian Friend
Sheila

Judge not; the workings of his brain
And of his heart – thou canst not see;
What looks to thy dim eyes a stain,
In God's pure light may only be,
A scar, brought from some well-orn field
Where thou wouldst only faint and yield

The look, the air, that puts thy sight,
May be a token here below
The soul has closed in deadly fight
With some infernal fiery foe,
Whose glance would scorch thy smiling grace
And cast thee shuddering on thy face!

And judge not lost; but wait and see,
With hopeful pity, not disdain;
The depth of the abyss may be
The measure of the height of pain
And love and glory that may raise
This soul to God in after days!*

---

* Written by my Father, Bert V. Wyatt, Dec 9, 1901

CONTENTS

PREFACE

everal years ago, this author completed an analytical quiz which was designed to identify a person's most prominent spiritual gifts. These turned out to be giving and exhortation. Gifts that are seemingly so different and yet so strangely synonymous when put into practice. It is hoped that both of these gifts are incorporated into the following pages to the fullest measure. An epilogue accompanying each poem has been constructed to provide the reader a scriptural thought and a glimpse into the author's thoughts. All of the Bible verses which seem to amplify the thought of each poem were gleaned from personal Bible study and from sermons, sometimes years after the poem was written. My prayer would be that these poetic thoughts induce an introspection by each reader, as they have the author to whom these thoughts were given. It is to this end that I commit these writings.

Mel Wyatt

INTRODUCTION

These poems, for the most part, provide a very solemn contrast between living and doing as the world does, and how we should live as people of God, being filled with the Spirit of God by what He did for us through the cross at Calvary. This contrast might better be defined by the words of our Lord that we read from the book of Jeremiah (Jeremiah 17 : 5-8).

"Thus says the Lord, "Cursed is the man who trusts in mankind and makes flesh his strength, and whose heart turns away from the Lord. "For he will be like a bush in the desert and will not see when prosperity comes, but will live in stony wastes in the wilderness, a land of salt without inhabitant.

"Blessed is the man who trusts in the Lord and whose trust is the Lord. "For he will be like a tree planted by the water, that extends its roots by a stream and will not fear when the heat comes; but its leaves will be green, and it will not be anxious in a year of draught nor cease to yield fruit."

The idol of self so frequently enters into the way of submission and obedience to the will of God. His will for us includes our having faith and trust and a willingness to wait for Him and His time to perfect us for His purpose. We should never cease praying for that moment in our lives.

ONE HALF OF DIALOGUE

Dialogue is defined
By a few of those who know
As not to words confined
Or feelings that we show

But feelings from a heart
From each and to each other
The self that we impart
As one to another

Dialogue is to love
Like blood is to the body
It hears the rhythm of
Another hearts melody

Grace is to dialogue
Like color is to art
Words from God's catalog
He enters in our heart

When Christians turn to pray
To our dear God above
He hears the words we say
And answers them with love

A poem oft displays
The poet's most inner mood
Much as an ode portrays
The feelings of an étude

When poets place their rhyme
Inked on a well worn scroll
Their verse is near sublime
A creation of their soul

And as these thoughts arrived
Which leave me quite agog
A poem, I derived
Is one half of dialogue.

Mel Wyatt

ONE HALF OF DIALOGUE

"Trust in Him at all times,
O people; pour out your heart before Him;
God is a refuge for us."
(Psalms 62:8)

"Speaking to one another in psalms and hymns
and spiritual songs, singing and making melody
with your heart to the Lord."
(Ephesians 5:19)

Day to day pours forth speech, and night to night
reveals knowledge.
(Psalm 19:2)

These words in poetry are the poet's half of dialogue with each reader. As you read each poem, your reaction and feelings will be the completion of this dialogue, and your spiritual feelings will be the completion of dialogue with your Lord.

THE BATON OF FAITH

We race along the path of life
Where God has placed us, everyone
And work and toil become our strife
But listen now my precious sons-

Let not your toil be everything
To family we must place our lot
And ever more to Christ our king
'Til when our self is long forgot

For self becomes a wall within
The door that would withhold our strength
If Christ our Lord cannot get in
And must remain "self's" distant length

Harken now for the hour is late
Each moment lost won't pass again
He is standing at "self's" locked gate
But only you can let Him in

Without His strength our race is lost
And life becomes a tangled mess
We must prepare and count the cost
And all our sins of self confess

And loose our pride that has such hold
That paralyzes our worship
For God has said we must be bold
And be in loving fellowship

Confess to Him and know the joy
Of life that's free from doubt within
And know His strength is our alloy
To help us run our race and win

The key is faith in what He said
And we must hear it from His word
That He desires to be our stead
And have our lives to Him deferred

The race is hard along life's path
A father's hope lies in his sons
Take from me the baton of faith
And then I'll know my race was won.

Mel Wyatt

THE BATON OF FAITH

"Do you not know that those who run in a race all run, but only one
receives the prize? Run in such a way that you may win."
(1 Corinthians 9:24)

'Behold, I stand at the door and knock; if anyone hears My voice and opens
the door, I will come in to him, and will dine with him, and he with Me.
(Revelation 3:20)

"I press on toward the goal for the prize of the upward
call of God in Christ Jesus."
(Philippians 3:14)

The thought of life being a race is quite common. All of the obstacles and hurdles
are set in place. Our motivations, however, and the banners we carry as we run the
race are proportional to our prize when we cross life's final finish line.

SUCCESS

There's a saying or a tale
And how it does apply
That the only time you fail
Is the last time you try

Plan your life to every turn
Well charted in advance
Read the map and no bridge burn
Leave naught at all to chance

But success seems to escape you
And makes you wonder why
You can't the things you want to
No matter how you try

A mystery of life revealed
To those who understand
That success is never sealed
Even tho it's always planned

Success is being in God's will
And His eternal love
Which makes our hearts fulfill
His guidance from above

A turning from our own desires
&Til we God's love possess
As the Holy Spirit inspires
And makes our hearts confess

That success is not in having
Or even how we must live
Success is not in getting
But in learning how to give.

Mel Wyatt

SUCCESS

"For the sun rises with a scorching wind and withers the grass; and its flower falls off, and the beauty of its appearance is destroyed; so too the rich man in the midst of his pursuits will fall away."

(James 1:11)

"In everything I showed you that by working hard in this manner you must help the weak and remember the words of the Lord Jesus, that He Himself said, "It is more blessed to give than to receive."

(Acts 20:35)

Success appears always to be related to some sort of measure. But is it a measure of wealth, or happiness, or only the fulfillment of desires? Success seems relative, and so it is, but when stripped of its worldly, rush-around definition, success loses its lustful implications and becomes a peaceful, attainable goal that all can humbly achieve.

HIS PEACE

Thru others acts we're sometimes pained
And must search for God's solution
For naught but loss is ever gained
Thru vindictive retribution

For hurt destroys when anger reigns
And "self" is Satan's victory
For he would amplify the pains
Then cast us to our destiny

Within self's black and lifeless void
Where hope is lost, self pity rules
Vindictive thoughts we can't avoid
Nor all of Satan's other tools

"Self" is Satan's lustrous trap
He lures us to our self made snare
And tells us "they" caused our mishap
Then leaves us without help to fare

Condemned by guilt, by self condemned
We're thrown into most deep despair
We find we can't on self depend
And feel there's no one else to care

We must confess our every thought
And pray for our hearts forgiving
T'ward any one we must hold naught
To be free again for living

God alone is true compassion
Our only guide to recovery
Look to Him and humbly fashion
The way that we should truly be

Thru help from Christ, our Savior King
As quietly to Him we pray
Loving praises our hearts should sing
With thanks for each and every day!

Beseeching Him to quell our hearts
For each hurt to be washed away
And thru His voice in inmost parts
Know that His peace is there to stay.

Mel Wyatt

HIS PEACE

"Thou wilt keep Him in perfect peace, whose mind
is stayed on Thee, because he trusteth in Thee."
(Isaiah 26:3)

"Peace I leave with you, my peace I give to you; not as
the world gives, do I give you. Let not your heart be
troubled, nor let it be fearful."
(John 14:27)

When we feel the pain of brother against brother or daughter against father or mother against son, or any person attacking another of God's creations, we must immediately identify the source of our pain and frustration and thoughts of vindication and look to the only one who can achieve a healing. Absolute humility and surrender will lead us to His peace. And when we forgive, and find it, we will be able to spend an eternity in perfect peace.

GOD'S GARDEN

The flowers in God's garden
Are like the flowers of spring
That lift their faces to Heaven
A haunting new hymn to sing

That love to be in the light
As morning dawns a new day
To be fully in God's sight
With petals open to pray

Refreshed by a voice within
Made new by the Spirit's dew
The flowers in God's garden
Are known as me and you

Unlike Satan's wilted tares
Bent, and without life or hope
Always knowing life's despairs
And denied the means to cope

But even Satan's flowers
If washed by the Spirit's dew
By the Holy Spirit's power
Can become God's flowers too

All flowers in God's garden
Can smile and need not frown
And the colors of His blossoms
Are black, and white, red, yellow
and brown.

Mel Wyatt

GOD'S GARDEN

"The wilderness and the desert will be glad, and the arabah will rejoice and blossom; like the crocus it will bloom profusely and rejoice with rejoicing and shout of joy . The glory of Lebanon will be given to it, the majesty of Carmel and Sharon. They will see the glory of the Lord, the majesty of God.
(Isiah 35:1)

"For you have forgotten the God of your salvation and have not remembered the rock of your refuge. Therefore you plant delightful plants and set them with vine slips of a strange God. In that day you plant it, you carefully fence it in, and in the morning you bring your seed to blossom; but the harvest will be a heap in the day of sickliness and incurable pain."
(Isiah 17:10&11)

"As for man, his days are like grass; as a flower of the field, so he flourishes."
(Psalms 103:15)

God created us all different and yet all the same in that we were created perfect in His sight. He created us to follow His light with our faces turned to Him, with the admonition that if we turn to worldly darkness we will be doomed. We can all be equated as flowers in God's garden, each with his own color, his own radiance, and his own special place where God has placed him to shine joy in His name and so become His praise.

FAITH

Faith is the captain on the battlefield
Faith is the shepherd of the band
Faith is our breastplate and our shield
Faith is the strength from the touch of God's hand

Faith is the healer of infirmity
Faith is knowing God hears and cares
Faith is the fulfiller of expectancy
Faith is power the Holy Spirit shares

Faith is hope emerging from fear
Faith is ever and always a must
Faith is the blotter that erases a tear
Faith is everlasting trust.

Mel Wyatt

FAITH

"Now faith is the assurance of things hoped for,
the conviction of things not seen."
(Hebrews 11:1)

Shown by many examples such as Noah, Abraham, and Moses, and described or defined by many words such as 'the doorway to hope' or 'the conviction that we need someone greater than ourselves'; yet this spiritual electrode, which enables a believer to be in contact with God's grace, is still one of man's greatest mysteries. Faith is too monumental to be defined by verse. Faith is the attitude given to man by the Holy Spirit which forms the synapses between himself and the grace of God which God wants to freely pour out on those who will accept this gift of the Holy Spirit. This synergetic relationship enables the dialogue between man and his Creator, and establishes the condition of being heir to God and so being able to claim all of the promises of God which He proclaims in His word.

A LUMP OF CLAY

The potter's wheel stands ready
To turn a lump of clay
The potter's hands are steady
So come and don't delay
  Dear Lord, hold me

The potter's hands are waiting
For clay that will submit
To their manipulating
Contrite, all sin to remit
  Dear Lord, mold me

Clay that resists the potter
That's dry and very stiff
Will soon begin to totter
And crumbles with a whiff
  Dear Lord, spare me

A figure now completed
From this little lump of clay
The fiery kiln now heated
To burn the dross away
  Dear Lord, refine me

The potter now rejoices
In silent admiration
Resound, you Heavenly voices
He's made a new creation!

Lord, hold me, mold me, spare me
Refine me I pray
For You are the potter and I am the clay.
       Mel Wyatt

A LUMP OF CLAY

"Behold, I belong to God like you;
I too have been formed out of the clay."
(Job 33:6)

Then I went down to the potter's house, and there he
was, making something on the wheel. But the
vessel that he was making of clay was spoiled in
the hand of the potter; so he remade it into
another vessel, as it pleased the potter to make.
(Jeremiah 18:3&4)

We must come to God with absolute surrender. Jesus said that we must come as little children. We indeed have to submit ourselves to Him as a lump of clay on a potter's wheel, ready to be formed into the perfect vessel that He would have us to be; a vessel created to carry His message of faith, joy, forgiveness and salvation wherever we are placed.

THE THORNY STEM

Within a thorny stem-
 God's tiny vessel - lies
A gift He gave to them
 To make them realize
All is not as it seems
 To sight or smell or touch
And if belief in dreams
 Or fantasies and such
Would only barely skim
 What man can analyze
The wonders done by Him
 Is what it magnifies
That God alone is great
 And His is all the power
On this earth to create
 A beautiful flower
A tree or something more
 A bush with scratchy thorn
That man would soon deplore
 As skin and clothes are torn
And everything that grows
 And man cannot condemn
Especially the rose
 From within the thorny stem.
       Mel Wyatt

THE THORNY STEM

"For it is written, 'I will destroy the wisdom of the wise,
and the cleverness of the clever I will set aside.'
Where is the wise man? Where is the scribe?
Where is the debater of this age? Has not God
made foolish the wisdom of the world?"
(1 Corinthians 1:19-20)

"But God has chosen the foolish things of the world
to shame the wise, and God has chosen the weak things
of the world to shame the things which are strong, and the
base things of the world and the despised, God has chosen,
the things that are not, that He might nullify the things
that are, that no man should boast before God."
1 Corinthians 1:27-29)

God did not create the world to confound man, but to prove His sovereignty; to dissuade us from seeking our own reason, and thus to continually seek His reason. So often we find ourselves confronted by persons or problems which seem to be a thorny stem in our lives. When this happens, we need to seek out God's reason, and, through prayer, discover the blessing that He has for us in these experiences.

STAND FIRM

Stand firm lest the war be lost
Stand firm and count the cost
Look up with eyes to the sky
Be assured of power from on high
Be aware of Satan's facade
Be entrenched in the word of God
Stay alert in days of strife
Stand firm with Christ in your life
Be filled with the Spirit's power
Make the war your shining hour
Stand firm when the arrows fly
Let praise be your battle cry
Be prepared for war's affliction
Stand firm in Christian conviction
Stand firm and count the cost
Stand firm lest the war be lost.

Mel Wyatt

STAND FIRM

"It was for freedom that Christ set us free;
Therefore keep standing firm and do not be
subject again to a yoke of slavery."
(Galations 5:1)

Only conduct yourselves in a manner worthy of the gospel
of Christ; so that whether I come and see you or remain absent,
I may hear of you that you are standing firm in one spirit, with
one mind striving together for the faith of the gospel; in no
way alarmed by your opponents--which is a sign of destruction
for them, but of salvation for you, and that too, from God.
(Philippians 1:27&28)

Stand firm therefore, having girded your loins with truth, and
having put on the breastplate of righteousness, and shod your
feet with the preparation of the gospel of peace; in addition
to all, taking up the shield of faith with which you will be able
to extinguish all the flaming missiles of the evil one.
(Ephesians 6:14-16)

Buzzwords like "new age" and "new world order" are being introduced into our vocabulary which appeal to man's intellect and would claim to be avenues for the institution of "world peace". In reality, the world is being conditioned for the fulfillment of the prophesies of the coming antichrist. Therefore, Christians must beware and be aware and stand firm lest we allow Satan's arrows to penetrate our armor and render us ineffective as Christ's disciples.

SUNDAY

They call it Sunday, and I wondered why
Did it come from a planet, a thing in the sky

And why not last, but first in the week
And why not rest, but pleasure we seek

For we know that the morrow awakens rude
And we wonder if we had an interlude
From the toils of life that we must go through
Because of the things we seek, and enough's too few

But Ah! There are greater things to seek
God sent the answer to this day in the week

He gave us His Son so that we might live
And asks no return that we could give
But a heart full of praise that's humble and meek
In return for SON DAY every day of the week.

Mel Wyatt

SUNDAY

"Then God blessed the seventh day and sanctified it,
because in it He rested from all His work
which God had created and made."
(Genesis 2:3)

For six days work may be done; but on the seventh day there is a
sabbath of complete rest, a holy convocation. You shall not do any
work; it is a sabbath to the Lord in all your dwellings.
(Leviticus 23:3)

We must frame this day within the golden border of God's intentions; that it becomes for us a day of dedication to rest and praise and worship and not just an extra day of the week for our indulgence in distractions.

GOD'S GRACE

Many mistakes are made each day
There's a chance with each decision
Many are made in a hasty way
While some are made with precision

Some are those we can't elude
As try and try we do
And some affect a multitude
While others only a few

Mistakes are big, mistakes are small
Mistakes are oft marked by tears
But the biggest mistake, I think, of all
Is succumbing to our fears

For God is here, our cares to take
And cast our fears aside
We know our trust He'll ne'er forsake
For us His only Son has died

This solemn act that some would grieve
And some would count for loss
Is full of grace, if we believe
The meaning of the cross.

Mel Wyatt

GOD'S GRACE

"For the wages of sin is death, but the gift of God
is eternal life in Christ Jesus our Lord.
(Romans 6:23)

"For the word of the cross is to those who are perishing
foolishness, but to us who are being saved it is the power of God."
(1 Corinthians 1:18)

We are so prone to label our sins--especially the little ones--mistakes. Praise God for His covering our sin in the way that only He could have done it. Praise God for the word of the cross!

A BUTTERFLY

As loved ones pass into God's arms
Our thoughts are turned to love
And memories of their loving charms
And praise to Him above

Who gave us moments we'll ne'er forget
Not even with passing time
And hearts that swell without regret
From memories sublime

The loss of loved ones renders strife
We ne'er can reason why
We only know, as a sign of life
God sent a butterfly.

Mel Wyatt

A BUTTERFLY

"For to this end Christ died and lived again,
that He might be Lord both of the dead and of the living."
(Romans 14:9)

"For this reason it says, 'Awake sleeper, and arise from
the dead, and Christ will shine on you."
(Ephesians 5:14)

Even for a Christian, the death of loved ones has a stillness about it; a time for grief of the loss, and yet a time also for reflection on past memories. It is a time also for knowing the nearness of God and for praising Him for the good news which tells us that death is really just the beginning of a more wonderful, eternal life for those who believe. Our dear Savior, Jesus, through His life, death, and resurrection, has been likened to a beautiful butterfly that has emerged gloriously transformed from a seemingly lifeless state. We praise God for this thought which helps free us from the pain of death.

MIRRORS

God gave us the joy
    Of His light divine
And has told us just how
    Our light should shine

We are saved by perfect
    Grace from above
And made as mirrors
    To reflect that love

To shine light to hearts
    Where darkness prevails
To shine courage and strength
    Where all else fails

To shine in dark alleys
    Where sin would hide
Reflections of hope
    Where hope doesn't abide

And as we're reflecting
    Let us be sure
That our mirror is clean
    And shining pure

Even crystal pure
    Oh that it might be
When we look in our glass
    'Tis Christ we see.

Mel Wyatt

MIRRORS

"For now we see in a mirror dimly, but then
face to face; Now I know in part, but then I shall
know fully just as I also have been fully known."
(1 Corinthians 13:12)

"Let your light shine before men in such a way that
they may see your good works, and glorify your
Father who is in Heaven."
(Matthew 5:16)

Arise, shine; for your light has come, and the glory
of the Lord has risen upon you. For behold, darkness will
cover the earth, and deep darkness the peoples; but the
Lord will rise upon you, and His glory will appear upon
you. And nations will come to your light, and kings
to the brightness of your rising.
(Isaiah 60:1-3)

The culmination of our prayers and our faith, having accepted God's glorious grace, is becoming aware of who we now are and what our re-created mission is as Christ dwells within us. This is where the Christian rubber hits the road as we let our light shine before men to the glory of God.

A GIFT

A gift all bound in golden wrap
Addressed to each and every one
Our names engraved upon the flap
A gift from God--His only Son

Only how do we receive it
Do we open it for our needs
Or do we only let it sit
For a time when our will concedes

Let this gift _be_ God's shining hour
His gift allows our souls to cope
Open His gift of grace and power
Be reconciled, receive your hope.

Mel Wyatt

A GIFT

"Every good thing bestowed and every perfect gift
is from above, coming down from the Father of lights,
with whom there is no variation, or shifting shadow."
(James 1:17)

"For God so loved the world, that He gave His only
begotten Son, that whoever believes in Him should
not perish, but have eternal life."
(John 3:16)

For a child will be born to us, a son will be given to us; and the government
will rest on His shoulders; and His name will be called Wonderful
Counselor, Mighty God, Eternal Father, Prince of Peace.
(Isiah 9:6)

At Christmas, people around the world are so taken up with giving and getting gifts that the true meaning is nearly obscured by this passion. We wonder at the enthusiasm with which this madness is pursued. Meanwhile, God, with all love and humility, is seeking a way into our hearts and minds to tell us about His gift, whom he sent to be the gift of life. Open God's gift and receive your salvation.

BEYOND THE CROSS

Beyond the cross where Jesus died
A place prepared by Him for all
A place believers will reside
When God, with trumpet, them will call
Thru you, oh death, all men must pass
Where each is stripped of human power
To step across your dark crevasse
Or even brave life's final hour
Without the strength from God above
Transcending as a golden ray
The radiance of agape love
The light of Christ to show the way
We trust, oh God, Thy glorious word
Which lights our path for all the way
And know our voices will be heard
When last upon our knees we pray
Lo, oh death, thy sting is fable
To those who know their journey's end
To those who trust that Christ enables
Each true believer to transcend
Oh death, for us you have no sting
Oh death, dark curtain that you are
Veil that covers life's beginning
Oh veil that hides the shining star
Oh death, with odor balmy sweet
When you should take me by my hand
And lead me to your barren street
Whose gate would mark the promised land
I'll not resist your chilling hold
And not consider life as loss
'Cause thru God's word we have been told
That life begins beyond the cross.

Mel Wyatt

BEYOND THE CROSS

"O death, where is your victory? O death, where is your sting?" The sting of death is sin, and the power of sin is the law; but thanks be to God, who gives us the victory through our Lord Jesus Christ.
(1 Corinthians 15:55-57)

"In my Father's house are many dwelling places;
if it were not so, I would have told you; For I go
to prepare a place for you."
(John 14:2)

"Jesus said to her, 'I am the resurrection and the life;
he who believes in me shall live even if he dies."
(John 11:25)

"Truly, truly, I say to you, he who hears my word, and
believes Him who sent me, has eternal life, and does not
come into judgment, but has passed out of death into life."
(John 5:24)

So many people are afraid of death and live almost with abandon to get the ultimate out of the few years that they know they have on earth amidst all the worldly pleasures. They call all of this success. Christians also need to look ahead to the end of their worldly life, not for worldly gain or with fear, but with a knowing that their time of doing God's will on earth has a physical termination. We should live as the apostle Paul wrote, "To live is Christ, and to die is gain." With this in mind, we know that we will live in the fullness of God on earth and be counted with the saints living in Heaven who pass eternity praising His holy name.

TO AN ANGEL

'Twas bitter pain upon his face
    The day that Enoch died
And grief shown there did not subside
    As thoughts went to that place

A father's tears would not hold back
    He could not find relief
Was it Satan's hand that caused his grief
    To sway him from God's track

If so, put Satan to the flight
    For Satan surely lied
And Enoch surely had not died
    He only joined the Light

And now he walks with God above
    As Enoch did of old
And he was taken, we are told
    Wrapped in the arms of love

So shout with joy that pain can cease
    Within our mortal soul
If we look upon a heavenly goal
    And trust in God for peace.

Mel Wyatt

TO AN ANGEL

"And Enoch walked with God; and he was
not for God took him."
(Genesis 5:24)

"Truly, truly, I say to you, that you will weep
and lament, but the world will rejoice: you will be
sorrowful, but your sorrow will be turned."
(John 16:20)

Believers are not exempt from tragedies in life, and have not been since man's first sin, when the serpent Satan began his quest for control of man's heart. Tragedies strike us without premonition and without understandable cause. Tragedies pierce our hearts like an arrow and inflict the same amount of pain. But, glory to God, though a scar remains, God's word gives us the means to pull the arrow out and heal the wound through the joy of a vision beyond the cross. Such a tragedy pierced this author's heart when our Christian daughter, "our love personified," was the victim of Satan's hand during a full-term still birth. They named him Enoch.

HOSPITAL CHAPLAINS

A chaplain knows and a chaplain
        weeps
But in his heart God's love he
        keeps
As he sees the hurts and knows the
        cares
God's love from within his heart he
        shares
To give them hope and God's loving
        peace
To quell their fears and their pain to
        ease
A ship of God, with God's wind in his
        sails
To renew his faith for weathering
        gales
May God yet give to him some
        rest
And knowledge that he is ever
        blessed.

                                Mel Wyatt

HOSPITAL CHAPLAINS

"Naked, and you clothed me; I was sick
and you visited me; I was in prison, and you came to me."
(Matthew 25:36)

"And the King will answer and say to them, 'Truly I say unto
you, to the extent that you did it to one of these brothers
of mine, even the least of them, you did it to me."
(Matthew 25:40)

"How blessed is he who considers the helpless;
The Lord will deliver him in a day of trouble."
(Psalms 41:1)

This poem, composed on my knee as I drove home from a prayer breakfast where the speaker was a hospital chaplain, is dedicated to those chaplains. All who are in the front line for the Lord are heroes in our hearts. May the Lord bless and keep them and give them His joy.

GRANDFATHER'S LAP

His hands were rough
And lines were etched upon his face
His shoulder was soft
And his arms were strong
His lap had become my favorite place

His eyes became white
When I was bad
His voice was sharp
When he said I was wrong
But when he smiled my heart was so glad

He has departed now
To Heaven above
But within my heart
I have a song
For I know that thru him I first learned love.

Mel Wyatt

GRANDFATHER'S LAP

"Grandchildren are the crown of old men,
And the glory of sons is their fathers."
(Proverbs 17:6)

"A gray head is a crown of glory; it is
found in the way of righteousness."
(Proverbs 16:31)

Children, obey your parents in the Lord, for this is right.
(Ephesians 6:1)

Family structures and values seem to be at the top of the world's hit list. Praise God for those parents and grandparents who will stand firm and not allow family values to erode. These thoughts were inspired by stories related about relationships with grandfathers, who were unswerving in their display of standing for what they believed, and yet so tender in understanding a child's feelings.

JOY

The world is seeking mirth and glee
That would seem to replace its strife
And all of its frivolity
Seems the cure for the woes of life

"Oh joy," they say, and party more
Free from responsibility
Abandon life and higher soar
Enjoy invincibility

Like planets soaring thru the sky
Out of control, so high and wide
With only self to satisfy
Without a thought they might collide

Satan has made a substitute
Every trick he does employ
To give to sin a high repute
And rob them of the real true joy

For sin and Satan are such thieves
Seeking to rob our joy divine
The joy each child of God receives
When from his heart God's light can shine

The world's joy is a shallow pool
Where pollutants of life may seep
The joy in Christ is water cool
From a well that is pure and deep

The joy of God which none can earn
That mirth and glee cannot replace
'Tis what Christ did that we must learn
To know the gospel and God's grace

To feel God's holy righteousness
Which He has given thru His love
That thru Christ's death we might possess
True joy that comes from Heav'n above.

Mel Wyatt

JOY

"Even in laughter the heart may be in pain, and
the end of joy may be grief."
(Proverbs 14:13)

"And the world is passing away, and also its lusts:
But the one who does the will of God abides forever."
(1 John 2:17)

"If you keep my commandments, you will abide in my love;
just as I have kept my Father's commandments, and abide in
His love. These things I have spoken to you, that my joy may
be in you, and that your joy may be made full."
(John 15:10&11)

What the world calls joy is often just a facade, a smiling face and macho behavior which would tend to hide the insecurities of anxiety and depression brought about by the inadequacies of self dependence. Christian joy, by comparison, is the realization of hope which is attained by faith and believing in all the promises of God. Christian joy is the knowledge of eternal life given by the good news of our Lord Jesus Christ. Christian joy is the heart-felt feeling that arrives from the giving of ourselves in appreciation for what Christ did for us. Christian joy is beyond the world's understanding.

WINTERS OF LIFE

Have you felt alone on a summer day
Felt as tho a loved one no longer cared
Have you felt the need to just sit and pray
Of a broken dream in a love you shared

Have you felt as tho life had passed you by
That no matter the game, you could not win
Have you felt the urge to just sit and cry
Or to find a river and just jump in

Do the rocks feel sharp on the path of life
As a love seems broken beyond repair
And the way is filled with the thorns of strife
Until all seems lost in complete despair

The winters of life are freezing storms
That could condemn our soul to destruction
If God is despised and our will conforms
To the course of our-own-ways construction

So please turn to prayer, you that have not heard
So that you might evade the thorns of strife
Always obeying your loving Gods word
To keep your soul safe thru winters of life.

Mel Wyatt

WINTERS OF LIFE

I am exceedingly afflicted; revive me, O Lord according to thy word.
(Psalm 119:107)

Blessed are the poor in spirit, for theirs is the kingdom of heaven.
Blessed are those who mourn , for they shall be comforted.
(Matthew 5:3&4)

Have I not wept for the one whose life is hard? Was not my soul grieved for the needy? When I expected good, evil came; when I waited for light, then darkness came. I am seething within and cannot relax; days of affliction confront me.
(Job 30:25-27)

This poem was the first of a quadruplet that were written in the shadow of tribulation when lifelong dreams were turning to sand and blowing away. Depression and despair are two of Satan's most vicious weapons; the victims of which feel lost and forsaken, much as Job must have felt. When life is fractured, the awareness of human frailty grips us and we truly understand then that we must seek God's strength because we are stripped of our means to cope. Know always that our God hears and answers prayers and that when we pray He works in such a beautiful way in our lives. Our sorrow allows us to experience the warmth and acceptance of a loving Saviour.

A LOVE THAT TOUCHES

Stripped of every earthly glory
Bare and naked I stand before Thee
Not knowing if my plight shall end
Not knowing what the future sends
    Only hoping by heaven above
    My heart can once again feel love
    As only You - Dear Heart - can bring
    The love that makes the angels sing
A love that smiles through all the clouds
A love that shines thru all life's shrouds
A love that touches when we're low
A love that leaves our hearts aglow
    A love that says it's not afraid
    When satan's bold attacks are made
    A love to share, a love to bring
    A joy that causes lips to sing
Alas! To dream of such a love
For such am I deserving of?
To trials of earth I shall be bound
In heaven alone can such be found.

Mel Wyatt

A LOVE THAT TOUCHES

And he said, "Naked I come from my mother's womb, and
naked I shall return there. The Lord gave and the Lord
has taken away. Blessed be the name of the Lord."
(Job 1:21)

There is no fear in love; but perfect love casts out fear, because fear
involves punishment, and the one who fears is not perfected in love.
(1 John 4:18)

Beloved, let us love one another, for love is from God; and
every one who loves is born of God and knows God. The one
who does not love does not know God, for God is love.
(1 John 4:7&8)

Ironically, the words of this poem were written the day before Valentine's
Day: the day when the world recognizes its kind of love. Yet even the fragrance
of a love comprised of feelings alone seems to escape us at times. We learn that
love from people is not dependable, that unforgiveness cannot be loved, and the
knowledge of broken trust turns our feelings to fear. Therefore, we must not let
satan have control, but turn to God's word where true love is revealed. The love
which touches, which can be felt by anyone who reaches out and asks.

PATHWAYS OF LIFE

Our paths might lead through valleys deep
Or over hills so high and steep
Always trails that lead somewhere
Seemingly there for those who dare

Some paths are strewn with stick and thorn
That lead to lust where souls are torn
Some paths are paved with golden bricks
And lined by Satan's other tricks

A pathway to heaven is there
A pathway of faith and of prayer
A pathway that Christ has prepared
Through grace, that our souls can be spared

And for those who would try somehow
To sail by "self's" light on their bow
And not by the shining Day Star
Will be lost and wander afar

On life's path we must look ahead
And use God's word to light our tread
For those looking back as they walk
Will stumble on every rock

If we fall and count not as loss
Losing sight of Christ's shining cross
Our doom is to know only strife
And sorrow's our pathway through life.

Mel Wyatt

PATHWAYS OF LIFE

Thou wilt make known to me the path of life; In thy presence
is fullness of joy; In thy right hand are pleasures forever.
(Psalm 16:11)

"He deprives of intelligence the chiefs of the earth's people,
and makes them wander in a pathless waste."
(Job 12:24)

Thy word is a lamp to my feet and a light to my path.
(Psalm 119:105)

"But if anyone walks in the night, he stumbles, because the light is not in him"
(John 11:10)

Every step taken on life's pathways is a challenge, every turn a decision. Sometimes we feel, as Moses must have felt, that there is no way through the wilderness of life. However, when we concentrate our focus on the Living Way, and let Him be our guide, the turns in our path seem to straighten. We should follow the words from Micah 6:8 which tells us, "He has told you, O man, what is good; and what does the Lord require of you but to do justice, to love kindness, and to walk humbly with your God?"

WAIT ON GOD

Does your heart feel saddened by sin
Is life overtaken by fear
Has pride been a monster within
Destroying the things you hold dear

Are you at the apparent end
With no hope at all in your view
Then know that God is your friend
And to wait is what you must do

He waits for us to wait on Him
He wants our hearts to wait and share
To wait 'til pride's loud voice grows dim
'Til when we come to Him in prayer

So lift your eyes to God above
And wait on Him to spread His wings
And catch you with His boundless love
To hold you 'til your sad heart sings

And then He'll help you fly again
And wait on you to gain your strength
To rid yourself of fear and sin
To fly for yet a greater length

Yes, wait on God to burn our dross
To clear our eyes and purge our thoughts
Renew our hearts as pride we toss
For He can do what we cannot

Pray for Gods judgment on our sin
For that is where His mercy is
Through humble hearts He can come in
To take our hearts and make us His.

Mel Wyatt

WAIT ON GOD

Indeed, while following the way of Thy judgments, O Lord, we have waited for Thee eagerly: Thy name, even Thy memory is the desire of our souls. At night my soul longs for Thee, indeed, my spirit within me seeks Thee diligently: for when the earth experiences Thy judgments the inhabitants of the world learn righteousness.
(Isiah 26:8&9)

Therefore the Lord longs to be gracious to you, and therefore He waits on high to have compassion on you. For the Lord is a God of justice: how blessed are all those who long for Him.
(Isiah 30:18)

Yet those who wait for the Lord will gain new strength: they will mount up with wings like eagles, they will run and not get tired, they will walk and not become weary.
(Isiah 40:31)

The Bible is full of God's exhorting His creation to have patience and to seek His help with all of our worldly problems. We are so prone to always try to find our own solution, and so inept to realize our inadequacies until all of our humanness is completely in our way. If we pray for wisdom or patience, the Lord takes us by the hand and leads us into His gymnasium and puts us on the machines so labeled and sends people and problems our way until our wisdom and patience are finally developed. In the meanwhile, He continually waits for us to wait on Him for the perfect solution to all of our needs and cares. But more especially, He waits on us to fully know Him as Sovereign King of our lives.

THE ESSENCE OF CHRIST

Through the stillness of death
    Christ comes to us
    Like silence in the night
Like the desert wind that
    stirs a cactus
    Eluding from our sight

Like the sweet fragrance of
    a desert bloom
    He dwells within our soul
Within our hearts He has
    prepared a room
    Our praises to extol

So be still my soul and
    listen for Him
    Let Him take possession
Let my failings and fears
    grow ever dim
    Through His consolation.

Mel Wyatt

THE ESSENCE OF CHRIST

"The wind blows where it wishes and you hear the sound
of it, but do not know where it comes from and where it is
going; so is everyone who is born of the spirit."
(John 3:8)

My soul waits in silence for God only; from Him is my salvation.
(Psalm 62:1)

Blessed be the God and Father of our Lord Jesus Christ, who has blessed
us with every spiritual blessing in the heavenly places in Christ,...
Which He brought about in Christ, when He raised Him from the
dead, and seated Him at His right hand in the heavenly places.
(Ephesians 1:3&20)

A golden thread woven through the book of Ephesians describes the "heavenly places". This is the spiritual realm where Christ resides. It is not, however, some distant place in the sky like we commonly vision heaven to be. It is rather the air around us. The space we occupy as we walk is surrounded by it. And we see that Satan, "the spiritual forces of wickedness", is there also. We must prepare our hearts and do as the Psalmist when he says, "My soul waits in silence for God only; From Him is my salvation". And we must remember always that only through Calvary's cross could Christ come to dwell with us and in us.

GAMBLERS

They'll never know the hand they're dealt
'Til the very last card is turned
With carefree feelings always felt
And no thoughts about bridges burned

They drift headlong thru all life's maze
And hurry as fast as they dare
They seek the most for all their days
Without stopping to pay the fare

Life's a gamble, they always say
As they tune out the church bell's ring
They'll bet on "self", let others pray
They don't need God for anything

Their ante is their very soul
As they put Christ's temple at stake
Hoping for an ace in the hole
And everything for it forsake

But when they're caught in Satan's snare
And "glitter" turns to days of strife
They say, in moans of deep despair
I guess this is my lot in life

Alas, when comes the final draw
And all of treasured life is lost
Our God will weep because He saw
That they never counted the cost.
                                    Mel Wyatt

GAMBLERS

The lot is cast into the lap, but its every decision is from the Lord.
(Proverbs 16:33)

He who trusts in his riches will fall, but the
righteous will flourish like the green leaf.
(Proverbs 11:28)

The wages of the righteous is life, the income of the wicked, punishment.
(Proverbs 10:16)

For the wages of sin is death, but the free gift of
God is eternal life in Christ Jesus our Lord.
(Romans 6:23)

"The church bell's ring" in this poem is symbolic of Gods presence in the physical realm of man's understanding. In our daily travels we pass by churches of all design and beauty, but unless people are present, they appear as though God was not at home. And so He isn't, until believers carry Him through the portals within their hearts to worship Him as one body. During a stay in Germany, I recall the church bells ringing all during the day, and how those stark edifices seemed alive with God's voice calling to His people. In my youth, the same ringing voices called to me and I would ride my bicycle and go to their calling as God's Spirit exhorted me to do. Today, God's voice, the living church, is threatened of being silenced by the world. With this stage set, it is natural that the person who does not know God's call should think - as the world thinks - that man's intelligence can prevail; and are willing to lose their lives taking that gamble.

LISTEN

Do you hear the whisper of breeze
As it softly moves thru the dell
As the leaves tittle on the trees
Lending voice to this magic spell

Do you hear God speaking to you
In the realm of His creation
When we see a majestic view
And come to the realization

God speaks to us in many ways
If we but listen for His voice
In nature's bliss where He portrays
These scenes which make our heart rejoice

His words are floating on the breeze
They echo from the canyon walls
They move in shadows under trees
From everywhere His glory calls

God grants us these windows of time
His way of entering our heart
Thru the Holy Spirit sublime
And once within, He'll not depart

'Tis God's way for Christ to enter
Heeding God's call we hold so dear
Keeping faith the very center
Listen in stillness, then we'll hear.

Mel Wyatt

LISTEN

In the beginning God created the heavens and the earth. And the earth
was formless and void, and darkness was over the surface of the deep;
and the Spirit of God was moving over the surface of the waters.
(Genesis 1:1&2)

In Him, you also, after listening to the message of truth, the
gospel of your salvation - having also believed, you were
sealed in Him with the Holy Spirit of promise.
(Ephesians 1:13)

Like an earring of gold and an ornament of fine
gold is a wise reprover to a listening ear.
(Proverbs 25:12)

As we spend our lives on earth - God's creation - and we are given a window
of time to stand in awe at the magnificent beauty of His handiwork, we must
always wait on God and watch and listen for the presence of the Holy Spirit.
As He was in the beginning, the Spirit of God yet moves over the surface of the
earth; and now the Spirit summons us to know God - to know Him as the triune
God who is all in all. It is only through the Holy Spirit that Christ also can enter
our heart. So be silent and listen and yield our hearts as the Holy Spirit beckons
to us in the beauty of creation to let God's love inundate us. It is only then that we
can fulfill our created destiny, which is to worship Him only. It is only then that
Christ Jesus can be our stead against mortal sin. It is only then that we can know
the fruit of the Spirit. It is only then that we can know the meaning of the cross.

LOVE

Love - is creation of the earth
Love - is a grandchild's simple smile
Love - is a mother giving birth
Love - is going that extra mile

Love - is a friendship when we're low
Love - is a hug that makes us glow

Love - is the giving of God's word
Love - is our home and family
Love - is the gift of our Saviour Lord
Love - was His dying at Calvary.

Mel Wyatt

LOVE

The one who does not love does not know God, for God is love.
(1 John 4:8)

We know love by this, that He laid down His life for us;
and we ought to lay down our lives for the brethren.
(1 John 3:16)

Love is patient, love is kind, and is not jealous; love does not
brag and is not arrogant, does not act unbecomingly; it does not
seek its own, is not provoked, does not take into account a wrong
suffered, does not rejoice in unrighteousness, but rejoices with
the truth; bears all things, endures all things. - - - But now abide
faith, hope, love, these three; but the greatest of these is love.
(1 Corinthians 13:4-7&13)

The Greek word for love in the verses from 1 Corinthians 13 is agape,
which characterizes God. This is the condition of love we are bound as
believers to try to emulate, but such that we could never duplicate. The
Greek word eros portrays love that shows feelings between a man and
woman, and the word phileo portrays love between friends. We see this
contrast between agape love and phileo in John 21:15-17, where Jesus
is asking Peter if he loves Him. Both types of love are denoted in the
question and Peter's answer. Many who read the "Love Chapter" do not
realize this important distinction and therefore extract a more rational
or emotional definition. Agape love is unselfish love. Agape love, as is
Christ's love for us, is undeserved and without price or recompense. We
could never replicate the cross; but because of agape love, we who believe
have become its beneficiaries. Praise God!

JESUS KNEW

Jesus knew - before His virgin birth
While He was yet with His Father
Creating the Heavens and earth,
He would be the Lamb for slaughter

Jesus knew - at the wedding feast
When He created wine from water
And healed the sick, at very least,
He would be the Lamb for slaughter

Jesus knew – when at priesthood age
As His mission on earth unfurled
To speak about great sacrilege
And repentance for the world

Jesus knew – they would not believe
That He would be the temple ram
Foretold Messiah sent to grieve
And be for sin, sacrificial Lamb

Jesus knew – and He was silent
When at trial He stood accused
And crowned with thorns before they went
Where He was whipped and cut and bruised

Jesus knew – it was for our iniquity
That He bore His cross to the hill
They nailed Him there for all to see
As a Lamb for our Father's will

Jesus knew – He'd die and rise again
Our Saviour, the great I AM
He did it ALL, just for our sin
God's perfect sacrificial Lamb.

Mel Wyatt

JESUS KNEW

In the beginning was the Word and the Word was with God, and
Word was God. He was in the beginning with God.
John 1:1&2

He was oppressed and He was afflicted, yet He did not open His mouth; like a lamb that is led
to slaughter and like a sheep that is silent before its shearer, so He did not open His mouth.
Isaiah 53:7

But Jesus kept silent. And the high priest said, "I adjure you by the living
God, thatYou tell us whetherYou are the Christ, the Son of God."
Matt 26:63

For it was the Father's good pleasure for all the fullness to dwell in Him, and through
Him to reconcile all things to Himself, having made peace through the blood of
His cross; through Him, I say, whether things on earth or things in heaven.
Colossians 1:19&20

'for all have sinned and fall short of the glory of God, being justified as a
gift by His grace through the redemption which is in Christ Jesus; whom
God displayed publicly as a propitiation in His blood through faith.
Romans 3:23-25

And they sang a new song, saying, "Worthy art Thou to take the book, and
to break its seals; for Thou wast slain, and didst purchase for God with thy
blood men from every tribe and tongue and people and nation.
Revelation 5:9

Printed in the United States
By Bookmasters